I0485398

The *Secrets* to Selling Your Home

A Real Estate Agent Reveals the Truth!

Intro

I can't take it anymore.

Home sellers are overwhelmed with information. Everyone has advice: agents, Zillow/Trulia, Homes.com, Craigslist, Realtor.com, Redfin, the neighbor, mom and dad, Uncle Jim.

A small amount of it is great stuff, most is well-known crap, and some is downright wrong or dishonest.

So, in this book, I'm going to have a cathartic purge. I'm going to lay it all out. A complete dump of my frustrations.

I'm going to answer your questions. Questions like...

- "What happens after I sign the contract?"

- "Where does my money go?"

- "Why is it so expensive to sell my home?"

- "What, specifically, is my agent doing to market my home?
- Is it a secret program?"
- "Is there a "standard" commission?"
- "Should I use a discount brokerage?"
- "Can't I just sell it myself?"
- "Why is an agent even necessary? What do agents really do, anyway?"
- "How much should I sell for?"
- Why does selling my home turn into such a stressful and painful experience? Shouldn't it be simpler?"
- And many more questions...

Most people don't have a clue to what really happens when they list their home with a real estate agent. Is there a secret book that tells the agent how to sell your home? A crystal-ball? Does the agent really know best?

What happens to all the money spent on selling your home? Is it really worth it? Could you have sold it yourself and saved a bundle? Do you really need to replace the carpet? Should you paint? Is finishing the basement a good idea?

I'll bet you've asked these questions before. Maybe the whole thing is still a mystery to you. The thing is, it shouldn't be.

Let's be honest, it isn't rocket science. Experience is important but there's nothing mysterious about selling a home. It's ALL about marketing and negotiating. But how much do you really know about how those things happen?

When you buy a car, a good salesperson looks for the things you are excited about. Whether the salesperson likes it or not isn't important. She wants you to crawl over every inch of it. To drive it. To smell it. Dare I say, to lust for it.

A good salesperson gets you to become emotional about that car and you begin to really, really want it! You want it so bad that you're willing to spend hundreds of dollars every month to drive that darn thing.

You believe that it's a good decision...AND you think you'll look cool in it! Why would a home be any different? We buy them on emotion as well.

Similarly, when you're the seller, you should be happy to pay the commission because you know it's a good financial decision! You clearly know that you are in the hands of a professional who is worth the money. This person will deal with the stress, frustrations, curve balls, arguments, complaints, negotiations, and many other torturous, eye-rolling issues. Anything short of that is unacceptable.

A quick intro about me. This won't take long and then we'll get to the juicy stuff...

Long before real estate, I was a United States Marine. As you can imagine, the Marine Corps teaches us how to complete our mission. My slogan is "When selling your home, I WILL complete my mission!" I put it everywhere to remind myself not to quit, not to slow down, not to be weak, not to whine, and to see the sale of your home as my mission.

The Marine Corps motto is "Semper Fidelis", which is Latin for "Always Faithful". Faithful to the corps, faithful to myself, faithful to you, and faithful to the mission.

If you want to see how I'm going to work for you, watch this clip of the death crawl from the movie "Facing the Giants"

[https://www.youtube.com/watch?v=-sUKoKQlEC4]

The most important question you'll ask me is:

"Are you going to give me your very best?"

So, in this book, I'm going to lay all the cards on the table. I'm showing you my hand. I want YOU to win big when you sell!

You'll read the fictional but common story of Joe and Maria Williams who are selling their home of 10 years and are wringing their hands trying to decide whether to try selling themselves and, if not, which agent to hire.

So, as Peter Pan says, "Here we go................"

The Williams Need a Bigger Home

Joe and Maria have three kids, a dog, and a goldfish. They live in Loveland, Colorado and they're hard working and happy. They love their community and living in Northern Colorado. They ski and mountain bike and love the outdoors.

Lately they've been talking about selling their home. They've been there for ten years. Their kids have made it all the way to high school in this home. They love it but it's too small now and they're busting the seams.

Joe owns an auto repair shop and Maria has been fortunate to stay home with the kids through their school years. Now she's thinking about cosmetology school and going back to work.

One night over spaghetti and meatballs, Joe says to Maria, "I think we need to sell the house and get something bigger." Maria responds, "You mean the kids don't have sleep in the closet now?"

Their youngest, Tyler says, "Wow, dad, I don't have to lay on the top shelf with your Star Wars miniatures collection now?"

"That's right gang, we're getting a house with two closets!"

Everyone cheers and just for a second, they think about a good old food fight. But…it's spaghetti, hello. Even so, the excitement is infectious…not unlike the flu they all had in the fall.

The next morning, Maria calls her yoga class friend Sandra, whose chiropractor's plumber knows a real estate agent. Maria figures a plumber ought to know something about real estate agents so surely that's a home run!

After her class and just as Maria is stepping into the shower, the real estate agent calls. She answers, and he says,
"Hi Maria! I'm Randal Ramey, the head of the Radical Ramey Real Estate team at Super Duper Realty and your friend Sandra's chiropractor's plumber told me to call you right away."

"Um, ok, that was fast but I'm a little tied up at the moment. Can you call back this evening when my husband is home?"

"I'm very busy but sure, what time?"

"About seven."

"Ok, that's a little late but I'll talk to you then. Radical Ramey out!"

"Ok, bye…I guess."

At dinner, Maria tells Joe that the agent is going to call at seven. So, after cheesecake for dessert, Joe jumps on the Internet and begins to research the Radical Ramey team.

"Hmmm. Randal works for a well-known company and has a team with the local office. That seems good."

"It says they've sold hundreds of homes and they've got a gazillion testimonials. I'm impressed! Sounds like a great choice."

About 7:15 PM, Joe's cell phone rings. It's Randal. He doesn't mention calling later than scheduled. Joe motions Maria over and puts the phone on speaker. Randal says hello and then launches right into…

"Mr. Williams, the company I work for has been around since 19 blah blah, I'm amazing, in fact, the whole team is amazing, and you'd be crazy not to list with me and I'll sell your home fast for the highest price, and…."

Joe and Maria listen to him talk without taking a breath for two minutes straight and are fairly impressed by that feat. Then, Maria butts in and asks, "How much do you charge, Randal?"

Randal answers, "Commissions are always negotiable, Maria, but I charge 6% for my services and let me tell you, it's well worth it!"

"Six percent, ok, but we're not sure what our home is worth—maybe $300,000 we think."

"No problem, I'll do a comparative market analysis. It's basically an appraisal."

"Hmmm, 6% would be $18,000. What do we get for that kind of money, Randal?"

Secret #1: Commissions are not set in stone. The real estate commission (Colorado Real Estate Commission in my state) prohibits setting a "standard" commission.

Randal says, "Well, I'm going to put it into the MLS with a bunch of photos I'll take with my smart phone. Then I'll post it to Zillow, Homes, Trulia, and Redfin so you'll get the greatest exposure."

"Ok, but what else for eighteen grand?"

"We'll put it in Homes and Land magazine."

"Yes, go on."

"And we'll put a nice little yard sign up for you with a phone number and a web site plus those cool information sheets!"

"Uh huh, the ones that get wet when it snows?"

"Ha, that's funny Maria. And I'll send it out to my vast network of agents who will surely bring us a buyer."

"And?"

"And we'll have some open houses."

Then Joe chimes in. "That's great but it still doesn't seem like it's worth that much money. What else to you do for that commission?"

"Oh, there's more! I'm going to show you how to make your house smell like chocolate chip cookies, I'm going to put balloons on the signs for the open houses, I'm going to negotiate the price for you, and I'm going to do ALL the paperwork!"

"Oh, wait, I'll give you a nice closing gift too."

Raised eyebrows commence.

Joe thinks to himself, "Wouldn't any real estate agent do all those things?" He covers the phone and leans over to Maria whispering, "Maybe we should interview a few different agents before deciding." Maria nods in agreement.

"Randal, we're going to interview a few agents before we decide but we'd like you to be one of them. Can you come over on Saturday at 10 AM?"

"Sure, but I'm a very busy guy with all the listings and sales you know so I can only spare about half an hour."

"Well, we'll try to keep it short." Joe feels a little uncomfortable with the time limit but figures it'll be okay.

Joe and Maria talk about the call a bit and come up with even more questions. Oh, well, tomorrow's another day.

During his lunch hour the next day, Joe calls a few brokerages and asks each one for their best agent to come and interview at their home on Saturday.

He figures he'll schedule them an hour and a half apart, so he and Maria have a chance to talk about each one in between interviews.

Since weekends are so busy for agents, he has a little trouble with schedules but in the end, gets it done. They'll have several agents to interview. They will compare each agent's services and make the logical choice. Simple.

Joe and Maria are a little anxious when Saturday morning rolls around, so they have decaf that morning.

Joe makes pancakes in various character shapes for the kids who get very excited about it, especially the Mickey Mouse pancakes. The funny part is that the kids are 15, 16, and 17 years old now but he's been doing this since they were two and they love it, so they won't let him stop.

Cute. He really doesn't mind and even insists on real maple syrup. Once the kids are off to their own activities for the day, Joe and Maria settle down for the interviews. Maria puts out some water, coffee, and tea just in time for the doorbell to ring.

"Sounds like Randal is here" says Joe. He goes to the door and invites Randal in. They all settle into the living room and Randal starts with small talk.

"You guys have a beautiful home here. How long did you say you've lived here?"

"Ten years", says Joe.

"We sell a lot of ten-year-old houses."

"Oh, hmmm, do you also sell younger or older homes?"

They all laugh…a little.

Feeling a bit awkward, Joe and Maria are glad when Randal says, "Well, let's get started, shall we?"

Maria offers him coffee, which he accepts. Then he lays a large binder on the coffee table facing them and turns to the first page.
"I just want to start by saying that after you see my listing presentation, I really can't imagine that you wouldn't want to list with me. So, let's do this!"

For the next hour, Randal "educates" them on his company, their history, why they're awesome, why he's awesome, throwing in a few attempts at humor along the way:

"Super Duper Realty has been around since 1953! We've sold almost as many homes as McDonald's has sold hamburgers! We have state of the art web sites and technology. We have tens of thousands of agents and offices in every major city in the U.S. Everyone has heard of us!"

"We have a huge convention every year where we go through extensive training for days, so we can get better at our jobs. We're members of the National Association of Realtors so we all have a Realtor® pin! Realtors® are held to a higher standard of ethics, you know."

"Our headquarters has over 50,000 square feet and hundreds of employees who are there to support us. We get tons of marketing materials branded with the company name and logo. Everyone knows who we are and we're very proud of that."

"Since 1953, we've grown from…."

"Our president and CEO says…"

"Our local office is known for…"

"My team's experience is…"

He goes on… "…" "…" "…"

After a while, he repeats what they heard on the phone about how he'll market their home. They were hoping to hear more this time. Joe and Maria listen politely but have a really hard time paying attention.

Soon, Randal starts to sound like the school teacher in the Charlie Brown cartoons: "Whah, whah, whah. Whah whah whah. Whah". An hour later, they say thank you to Randal and compliment him on his "great presentation".

Randal says, "Great, so let's get this listing agreement signed and get started!"

Maria elbows Joe who says, "Well, we want to think about it and we have a few other interviews to do anyway. We'll let you know next week."

Secret #2: Most agents still don't understand that clients don't care much about the size of our company, how many awards we have, how much is spent on national marketing, or a bunch of other stuff. That may have been true 60 or 70 years ago, but today it's different. Clients want to know how the agent is going to deliver. Things like:

"What do I get for my money?" "Why should I choose you (not your company)?" "What value are you providing me?"

Randal presses a bit more but finally caves and says, "Ok, but remember, we're the best. We'll get you the highest price and sell in the quickest time! Call me!"

Tip: This is known as a "call to action", a common sales tool.

They walk him to the door just as the agent scheduled for the next interview is walking up. Joe and Maria realize she's twenty minutes early and not knowing how to act, say goodbye to Randal without mentioning to the agent walking to their door, that Randal is also an agent. They imply he's a friend or relative.

It doesn't work because Randal's dressed up, carrying a bag full of work stuff, and as he reaches his car, again calls out, "Call me! I'll sell it for you, I promise!"

"Well, that wasn't awkward at all", Maria says. Joe shrugs.

The next three interviews go basically the same way. All the agents seem fixated on their credentials, company, and getting a listing agreement signed. Joe and Maria have no idea what kind of black hole their $18,000 in commissions would go into, but they do know that nothing ever comes back out.

A little discouraged, they slump through the rest of the weekend. What now?

On Monday, the sun is shining, and Maria walks out to get the mail. She begins to sort the junk mail out when she notices a simple post card with the words:

Need a bigger home?

www.StartPackingToMove.com

Or call David Mac at 970.703.4040

Sellstate Crossroads Realty, Loveland, Colorado

That's all it said. No photo. No names. Nothing except the brokerage name.

Maria thinks, "Huh, I wonder what's at the website? Maybe we can find out what the house is worth without talking to another weirdo agent."

She types in the URL on her laptop and a photo of a beautiful home fills the page. In the middle are the words "How Much Is Your Northern Colorado Home Worth?" and a box to type in an address. She shrugs, types hers in and hits enter.

The next page asks three simple questions. In a few seconds, there's a simple report stating that her home is worth $312, 590.

There's a little chart showing the trend in value over the last several years, a list of comparables, and a few details about her property. She stares at it and thinks, "That was easy."

Near the bottom, she sees "Thank you for requesting a CMA for your home. Visit my other site: www.DavidSellsNOCO.com for more information about my High Premium Home Listing Service.

She shrugs again and clicks on the link. A page on a web site for Sellstate Crossroads Realty pops up with the photo of a really, really, ridiculously good-looking guy named David McCullough.

She has trouble paying attention to the rest of the site because the photo is so mesmerizing. Finally, against her will, she forces herself to look around.

While it's a pretty standard real estate site, the page she has landed on looks VERY INTERESTING! She thinks, "Maybe we should call David and see if he's any different from the cookie cutter clan."

When Joe gets home, Maria tells him the story and shows him the web site and David's photo. He looks around and says, "What the heck, give him a call."

Maria, still staring at David's photo, says, "You better call him, I'm feeling light-headed." Joe looks at her with confusion and agrees to make the call.

Joe calls at 8 PM and David answers. This seems promising. Joe says, "Hi, David, my wife got your postcard and found your web site. We'd like to talk to you about your listing services. So far, we're not very encouraged so absolutely no promises."

"Sure, Joe, I do listing appointments by appointment Tuesday through Friday from 2 PM to 8 PM. I have openings on Tuesday at 3 PM and Wednesday at 5 PM. Will either of those work for the two of you?"

"Well, I don't get home until five, could you meet us Wednesday at 5:30 PM?"

"That will work", David replies. "Ok, see you and Maria Wednesday at 5:30 PM. What's the address?"

Joe gives him the address and then says, "David, we're not signing anything that night."

"No problem, Joe. My goal is to provide the highest possible value to you and Maria. That's all."

"Ok", Joe says, "We'll see you then." Joe hangs up and tells Maria how he feels good about this one.

When the appointment finally rolls around, David shows up at 5:25 PM. He knows that too early is just as bad as too late for this kind of appointment. Don't want to rush them and don't want to be inconsiderate either.

David shows up with a folder holding a note pad and a pen. Nothing else. After a brief hello, Joe and Maria show David to the living room and as David is walking past the family pictures, he comments on the kids. "If you don't mind me asking, what are the kids' names?"

Moms are so proud of their children. Maria points to each photo and says, "Tyler, James, and Mariana."

"And their ages?" David asks.

"17, 16, and 14."

"Wow, you guys had your kids close together like my wife and I did."

"How many children do you have, David?" Maria asks.

"We have three as well, 32, 31, and 30. We also have five grandchildren, all seven and younger. They grow up fast, don't they Maria?"

"Yes, they do", she responds.

Joe and Maria are feeling pretty good about this so far. Maria motions to a spot where David can sit down, and she and Joe sit opposite of him.

David lays the pad of paper and pen down and continues to chat.
"Have you guys always lived here in Loveland?"

"No, we're originally from California" says Joe.

"Oh, what part?"

"San Diego."

"Wow, small world, I'm from just east of Los Angeles. I've been in Colorado for 23 years though, so our kids grew up here."

"Yeah, us too. We've been here since 2000 so it's home."

"Do you still have family in California?", David asks.

"Yeah, Maria does, and I have a brother there."

David says, "Most of my family is there too but I got tired of the crowds and traffic. I just had to get out."

"Yep, we get that", says Maria.

This goes on for about five minutes as David gets to know Joe and Maria better and vice versa. Then David says, "So why are you guys considering selling?" He picks up the yellow pad and pen and begins taking notes.

Joe answers, "We've outgrown the house now. We need more space for the high schoolers who think they need, quote, privacy."

David laughs. "We know *all* about that. It's what happens before they fly away completely, and you end up empty nesters."

He continues. "I'll bet you've got a lot of memories here though."

"Well, that's true. We've made it a home and I'm sure the kids will miss it."

"I'll bet you'll miss it too, Maria."

"You're right. Lots of good times here."

David adds, "My wife and I are actually in the process of selling our own home right now. We need to downsize but it's kind of hard to leave."

He continues, "Sometimes I still hear the kids' voices in the basement, yet there's no one there but us. I'm either nostalgic or crazy."

Joe and Maria nod as if they see their future.

David turns to Joe. "So, what do you do for a living, Joe?"

"I own an auto repair shop in Fort Collins."

An entrepreneur! I love small business. "Do you want to move to Fort Collins?"

"No, we love it here in Loveland, we just need a bigger place."
"So, your 'why' is about getting more space? Your family needs more room to stretch out and the kids need some privacy. I'll bet at 14, Mariana is really feeling that."

"Yep. Sharing a bathroom with the boys is getting stressful", says Maria.

"We have a boy and two girls, so I get it", David says.

"Do you work outside the home, Maria?"

"No, but now that the kids are older, I'm considering it. Maybe cosmetology or something in the beauty industry."

"Great, I need a facial and a haircut. Wanna practice on me tonight?"

"Ha, I don't think you'd want that quite yet."

"Couldn't be any worse than my current barber. I mean, look at me!"

They all laugh and chat. Soon, David says, "Well, we better get down to business or we'll be here all night."

Joe says, "Alright, let's."

Everyone's Favorite Radio Station

Radio Station WIIFM

Joe says, "So, David, I kind of like you so far but we've already interviewed four agents and I gotta tell ya, they didn't impress us."

"Why is that?", David asks.

"Well, they talked up their companies and their services, but we just didn't feel like there was a connection."

"That could be because they listen to the wrong radio station."

"Huh?", Joe says.

"Well", David says, "everyone's favorite radio station is **WIIFM.**"

Joe and Maria look at David and then each other, then back at David.

"Ok, you've lost me", Joe says as he stares at David with confusion.

"Joe, you and Maria are very nice people, but the reason you guys are talking to a real estate agent is to answer the question: 'What's In It For Me?'. That's the radio station, WIIFM".

"We're all that way", David adds.

"Go on.", Joe says with raised eyebrows.

"Sales people tend to parrot what they've been taught. What if I were giving a formal presentation at a board meeting for Coca Cola? I might want to talk a little about the firm I work for because Coca Cola isn't likely to go into business with a company that started up Friday afternoon."

"But I'm not talking to Coca Cola, I'm talking to you."

Things like the size of the brokerage I work for, the four-color brochures they provide us, and the conventions we go to mean nothing to you guys."

"You want to sell your home, right?"

"Yeah."

"So, I want to talk about that."

"How you've got memories here and it's hard to leave. Your concerns about pricing and the market. About the huge pile of money called commission and what it buys you."

"About how much equity you'll net and whether it's enough to get you into a bigger place. About how your kids will feel about all of this. Will they have to change schools? Teams? Youth Groups?"

"We need to talk about your 'why' and your concerns, not about the credit rating of the parent company of our brokerage. Of course, you want to know that you're working with someone who's experienced in the real estate business and working with a reputable brokerage but it's not as important as the WIIFM station you're tuned into."

"So, lay it all on me. All the doubts, fears, concerns. Once we get past that, we can talk about how to sell your home. In short, you tell me the 'why' and I'll take care of the 'how'."

Maria just stares. "No one else has talked to us that way."

Joe winces and agrees. "Yeah, I'm not sure about you."

"Ha ha, well I hope I'm making sense. All I'm saying is that your 'why' and your concerns have to be settled first and then the rest is simple."

"Ok, David, I'm think I'm pickin' up what you're layin' down. We know why we're selling. Now tell us how you'd sell our home. Then, we'll see if you're legit."

"Ok, fair enough. If your concerns are settled to this point, behold the marketing plan…"

"Joe, Maria, in military jargon, real estate agents are snipers and you're the high value target. Don't panic, no guns are involved. Yet."

"Kidding.

"First, let's cover the things EVERY agent should be doing when listing your home. These are the cookie cutter, standard, and typical services you'd expect.

"Of course, your home will be listed in the MLS. Now, in our area, there are two MLSs we need to be concerned about: IRES and REColorado."

"IRES covers all of NOCO down to Broomfield and Boulder where it begins to overlap with REColorado, which services all of Denver metro and the surrounding cities."

"In order for agents in the Denver area to have access to your listing information, we'll place it in REColorado as well as IRES."

That's a huge number of agents seeing your listing because IRES has 6,000 agents and REColorado has 20,000(!), so we definitely want the Denver market to know about your home! Lots of commuters these days."

"Next, because I work for Sellstate, we have a direct feed to Zillow, Realtor.com, Trulia and a ton of other sites that 'syndicate' our listing information. Direct feed means they pull our listing information and display it on their own sites."

"But David, I've heard that Zillow and other sites like it don't have accurate data."

"You're right, sometimes they don't stay caught up."

"But that's not true in our case."

"The deal we have with them is for a DIRECT feed from the MLS. That way, the information about your listing is always up-to-date and accurate. Millions of people all over the country can see the correct info at all times."

"Well, ok then! Nice", Joe remarks.

"Of course, I'll let all of our agents know about your listing and I'll profile it in our sales meetings so that the entire office is mobilized and looking for the ideal buyer. I'll also email it out to every agent in my database so they all know it's available."

"Sounds good", says Maria.

"I'll put a listing sign in the yard and a lockbox on the front door."

"Uh huh. What else."

"We'll do a couple of open houses."

Maria looks at Joe with a "This sounds familiar" look.

"Go on", Joe prods.

"That's it", says David

"Seriously, for $18,000 or more, that's all we get?", Joe asks.

"Yep", David quips.

"Frankly, David, we thought you'd be different."

David pauses for a second for dramatic effect and then says, "Ok, ok, sorry. I'm having a little fun here."

"There's much more and I will lay out the rest of my marketing plan shortly, but my point is that most agents stop there. They feel like they're doing what they promised to do, and this is what they were taught."

"Now, let me run you through what happens after you sign the *typical* listing agreement. This will be educational. Then, I'll circle back around and explain how I do things!"

The Average Agent, Yawn.

"Ok, first of all, when you say yes to a listing agreement, the agent nearly has an aneurysm because she 'got one'. Then some documents are slid over or emailed for you to sign."

"You sign the **Exclusive Right to Sell Listing Agreement** and some disclosures. The agent gives you a packet with some tips about curb appeal and making the house smell good."

"The agent whips out their cell phone and starts snapping photos of your home while giving you tips on sprucing things up."

"They promise the moon, tell you how excited they are, pounds a scratched-up sign into your yard, and puts the lockbox they bought at Lowes on the front doorknob."

"You're instructed to paint, replace the carpet, pull weeds, cut the grass, and put some plants out on the porch—if yours is the average home."

"And the secret weapon: make the home smell good by baking cookies before every showing."

"Then, they will float out of your house on their invisible magic carpet while giving themselves high fives and counting their cut of the commission in their head."

"So, when you say goodbye, they hardly notice."

"Back at the office, everyone says, 'Congrats on the new listing! You're a rock star! Keep it up!' while being secretly jealous and cussing the agent under their collective breath."

"Then the agent wanders back to her desk and fires up the MLS. The listing info is typed in and it goes live with about 30 minutes work."

"The MLS syndicates it out to all the Internet sites like Zillow, which takes very little work."

"Since it's 2 PM now, they head to the bar where they will spend half their commission celebrating and thinks, 'I love my job!'"

"The agent answers the phone a few times during the next weeks to confirm showings by buyers' agents and prints some flyers for Saturday's open house. The open house is from 1pm to 3pm with about 20 minutes of drive time each way."

"Your listing might go into the newspaper, Homes & Land magazine, and on Craigslist. Maybe."

"After this, they move on to other 'deals' while waiting for the right buyer to make an offer on your home. So far, the agent has about five hours invested."

"Then, as a few solid offers come in, the listing agent calls and says, 'Let's go over these offers and choose the best one.' That takes an hour plus drive time."

"You choose an offer based on their advice and they then call the buyer's agent with the good news. Everyone signs and you're now under contract."

"Then comes an inspection and an appraisal. That usually takes little to no time invested by the listing agent."

"Maybe there are a few questions about the loan conditions or appraisal results, then a couple of pieces of paper are shuffled back and forth."

"In most transactions, the listing agent might have to recommend you have a few repairs done due to the inspection objection from the buyer."

"There could be other issues with title or appraisal and the agent will mention how hard they worked to solve the problems. You can practically hear their sweat over the phone."

"Once that's all ironed out, everyone waits until the day of closing. Everyone shows up, exchanges pleasantries, gets free coffee and a pen, signs a boatload of cryptic documents, and finally--close the transaction. Then, they all walk out of each other's lives."

"So, that's another few hours but let's be generous and say five. Together that makes 10 hours invested in selling your home."

"Phew. Wipe the sweat from my brow. You'll probably get some sort of not-too-expensive 'closing gift' too to prove how much you're appreciated."

"10 hours of work? That's it?", Joe exclaims. So, why does it cost so much?"

"Well, to be fair to my fellow agents, it's just how things have always been done. Have you ever heard the story of the Thanksgiving ham?"

"I don't think so", says Maria.

"Well, I actually lived this very story myself. Here's how it goes:"

"A newly married couple were cooking their first Thanksgiving ham together. The husband noticed that his new wife cut off both ends of the ham before placing it in the baking pan."

"He asked her why she did that and after thinking about it for a moment, she said, 'I don't know, actually, my mom always did it that way. I'll call and ask her."

"So, she calls her mother and asks her why. Her mom pauses for a second and then says, 'Well, honey, when my mother was making Thanksgiving ham, the pan was too small to put it in whole, so she cut off the ends to make it fit."

"So, the lesson, of course, is that just because we've always done something a certain way, doesn't mean it makes sense to keep doing it."

"Real estate agents are no different and most keep doing 'what's always worked'. But times have changed." Even so, let's be fair and break it down from their point of view."

"First of all, the listing agent doesn't know if the first buyer will work out. It could be—and often is—the second, third, or even fourth buyer who gets to the closing table. So, the listing agent's hours begin to multiply. So that's one thing."

"Secondly, the listing agent only keeps half of the commission. The other half goes to the buyer's agent who succeeds in bringing the right buyer."

"Third, if the listing agent is doing their job, there can be significant expenses in marketing a home well. It could be 25% or more of the listing agent's part of the commission."

"Once an agent does close a transaction, the broker they work for wants their cut also, usually anywhere from 10% to 50% of the listing agent's half! After all that, the agent has other expenses not directly related to your particular home such as gas, oil, car washes, maintenance, etc."

"Then there are marketing costs to find a seller/buyer in the first place. Lots of direct mail usually. Agents have web sites, automated email services, MLS fees, insurance premiums, Realtor board fees, office fees, printing costs, lockboxes, signs, and the list goes on."

"Real estate agents are self-employed, so they have self-employment tax, Medicare tax, and income tax for federal and state agencies."

"I assume you see the point. It ain't cheap to be in real estate. In the end, the agent doesn't keep nearly as much as you think."

"Let's do the math on a $300,000 home."

"We'll use the common charge of 6%."

"6% of $300,000 = $18,000."

"Half of $18,000 is $9,000, which goes to the listing brokerage."

"The brokerage gets its cut. Could be 20% of the $9,000, so the listing agent is left with $7,200. It all depends on the company's agreement with the agent. Some are fantastic, and some are not so good, but we'll stick with 20%."

"Out of $7,200, the agent has marketing expenses directly related to your home, let's say 10% or $720, leaving $6,480."

"Then, the agent pays some percentage of what's left for taxes, insurance, lead generation, auto expenses, office fees, etc. Let's say that's $1,200. As you know, Joe, self-employment tax by itself is 15.3%."

"So, regardless of how many hours an agent works on selling your home, the agent is left with $5,280. That's a long way from the 6%/$18,000 you see in the listing agreement."

"But I completely understand that this doesn't make it any less painful for the seller coughing it up."

"I understand that but I'm going to help make you feel a lot better about it. Still, I don't fault any agent for charging their preferred commission. I really do feel like it's worth it to sell your home. "

"But…I also don't believe listing agents *do enough* for you. Ten hours isn't much time invested."

> Secret #3: "Agents joke about how little time they put into listings. Your listing is considered the 'Holy Grail' of appointments. Listing agents hire buyer agents to do showings, so they don't have to do that part themselves."

"Now, I'm not trying to throw them under the bus. I do know some excellent agents who do a terrific job for their clients. None of this is meant to put them down."

"Plus, as of the writing of this book, Colorado's market is on fire! IRES (an MLS service) reported that for Jan 2017, the average days on the market until an offer came in was seven! Seven days to be potentially be under contract. That's fast!"

"I've experienced this myself many times. For example, I listed a house on December 29th, 2017. I placed the sign in the yard on December 30th, 2017."

"It was under contract—for more than the asking price—by Sunday night, December 31st, 2017, less than 24 hours!"

"Translation: In this market, a monkey could sell your home."

"So, maybe we should just sell it ourselves", Joe chimes in.

"Sure, you can do that, and some people do. But you might want to look at these statistics from the National Association of Realtors first."

David shows them a page from the NAR website:

For Sale by Owner (FSBO) Statistics

- FSBOs accounted for 8% of home sales in 2015.

- The typical FSBO home sold for $185,000 compared to $240,000 for agent-assisted home sales.

- FSBO methods used to market home:

  • Yard sign: 33%

  • Friends, relatives, or neighbors: 21%

  • Online classified advertisements: 10%

  • Open house: 21%

  • For-sale-by-owner websites: 7%

  • Social networking websites (e.g. Facebook, Twitter, etc.): 9%

  • Multiple Listing Service (MLS) website: 13%

  • Print newspaper advertisement: 3%

  • Direct mail (flyers, postcards, etc.): 2%

- *Video: 1%*

- *None: Did not actively market home: 41%*

- *Most difficult tasks for FSBO sellers:*

- *Getting the right price: 18%*

- *Preparing/fixing up home for sale: 13%*

- *Understanding and performing paperwork: 12%*

- *Selling within the planned length of time: 3%*

- *Having enough time to devote to all aspects of the sale: 3%*

Source: https://www.nar.realtor/research-and-statistics/quick-real-estate-statistics

"Let's do the math. Assume a $300,000 sales price with a listing agent."

"Subtract $200,000 for the existing mortgage payoff."

"So, we have $100,000 and we subtract the commission of $18,000. That leaves you with **$82,000** using an agent."

"According to NAR's statistics, the FSBO would bring 77.9% as much as using an agent. That's $231,300. Subtract the mortgage payoff and you're left with **$31,000**."

"$31,000 versus $82,000 and you get to do all the work."

"So, while you could do it…well, I think you get the point. In the current market, listings are getting multiple offers FAST. Some are over asking price right out of the gate! So, we might as well focus on getting all we can quickly."

"Ok, David, you've been running your mouth for ten minutes. Can I ask a question at this point?"

"No."

"Kidding. Sorry, I get excited about what I'm doing for clients. I love it! What's the question?"

"You think you're funny, don't you? My question is, 'Do you know any monkeys that can sell our home?"

"Good one! Excuse me, could you pass me that banana please Thank you, I'll be here all week. But seriously folks, beyond the things we've talked about, there are several other reasons to use a real estate agent."

Secret #4: You can sell your home yourself as a FSBO but according to the National Association of Realtors: "The typical FSBO home sold for $185,000 compared to $240,000 for agent-assisted home sales", 22.9% less money.

Note: There is criticism of this statistic that, I believe, is valid. Even so, there are other reasons to use a Realtor®.

"The most important reason is that I am licensed with the Colorado Real Estate Commission and I carry errors and omissions insurance."

"There's also:"

- Knowledge
- Experience
- Negotiating
- Transaction management
- Contracts and disclosures
- Control of who is tromping through your home
- Filtering out those who aren't serious or can't afford it."

"There's more but…"

Maria asks, "Ok, we get it, but what about one of those discount brokers? If it's so easy to sell in this market, why don't we just pay one of them 500 bucks to put our house in the MLS?"

"Ah yes, the discount broker", David says.

"Ya know, that's very similar to just selling it yourself. I certainly have nothing against those brokers. They have every right to sell their service."

"But, you need to know exactly what you're getting and then, if that's what you want, go for it."

"Let's take one example, the 'Flat Fee' model. This type of service advertises a flat fee for the listing service. Let's use $500 as an example. It seems like you can sell your home and it will only cost you $500. That's how it's often marketed."

"But, that's misleading. It won't include the buyer's agent fee. It's hard to get buyer's agents to bring buyers if you don't pay them. So, for that you can add 2% to 3% to the sales price."

"So, using 2.5%, we have $7,500. Add that to your flat fee and your total is $8,000 or so, not $500. While that is still a savings, the listing agent won't likely be as active in the process."

"It really depends on what you're comfortable with. If you've sold homes yourself before, it could be an option for you. NAR's more general home seller statistics for 2015 are the following:"

> *• 89% of sellers were assisted by a real estate agent when selling their home.*
>
> *• Recent sellers typically sold their homes for 98% of the listing price, and 37% reported reducing the asking price at least once.*
>
> *• The typical home sold was on the market for 4 weeks.*
>
> *• 64% of sellers who used a real estate agent found their agents through a referral by friends or family, and 25% used the agent they previously worked with to buy or sell a home.*
>
> *• Sellers who definitely would use same agent again: 70%*

Source:https://www.nar.realtor/research-and-statistics/quick-real-estate-statistics

"So, if you believe that you're comfortable in that top 11% of sellers who sell their own homes in some fashion, do it. But if not, I'd like to help."

<u>"Let me take on all the stress, anxiety, and pain for you."</u>

> *Secret #5: If you've bought or sold a home through a real estate agent before, you know what an emotionally draining experience it can be. Consider how much more so if you do everything yourself.*

"And speaking of FSBO, <u>if you do go that route</u>, I have a proposition for you."

- I'll put a professional "For Sale by Owner" sign in your yard.

- Interested buyers will call a toll-free number that I provide on the sign and hear all the details they want including the price!

- They'll call me if they're interested and I'll ask a few pre-qualifying questions before I send them over to you. This way you won't have to waste time with people who aren't really buyers.

- I'll also advertise your home on its own web site and I'll send buyers to it with focused online advertising.

"You'll have tons of potential buyers, but you won't have to talk to any of them until the offers start pouring in! And the price for all this?"

"Free."

"That's one of the best four-letter words in the English language. How can I do this? WHY would I do this? I must be crazy, right?"

Joe sneers a bit and asks, "C'mon, David, what's the catch? What do you get out of it?"

David answers calmly, "Actually, I do get something out of it."

"Most people I talk to won't buy your home, but I still make contacts who might buy or sell another property with me in the future."

"Neighbors notice the professional marketing effort (free advertising) and become curious. Some of them become clients."

"If you bring the buyer, it costs you nothing. I'll consider it good will for any transactions or referrals you send my way later."

"If I do bring a buyer to you, only then would I ask you to pay a 3% commission. I'll do the paperwork and closing for you."

"You're happy, I'm happy, and you'll remember me. This is worth a lot to me in the long run. Promoting my service is my goal. In my opinion, it's a win-win."

Maria studies the idea quite a bit and says to Joe, "I don't see a down side here."

- "If he sells the house for us, we get full service for our money."

- "If we sell it ourselves and David brings the buyer, we only pay for the buyer side. That's half as much."

- "If we sell it ourselves and we bring the buyer, we pay nothing."

"Is that about right, David?"

"That's exactly it, Maria."

"And you pay for the sign, the website, and the advertising? You take the phone calls and do the paperwork?"

"Yep."

"Well, you couldn't make that any simpler for us. We'll definitely consider it if we decide to sell it ourselves."

Pricing Your Home to Sell

Joe's been a little quiet to this point, so David asks him, "What are you thinking about, Joe?"

Joe looks up and answers, "Oh, I'm just taking it all in. I mean, this all sounds really good but there is still one major issue we haven't talked about: **what price to list it at**."

"I expected that to come up, Joe" says David. "Let's go over the critical step of choosing the best price at which we should list your home."

"Sounds good", Joe says. Maria nods in agreement.

"Price is probably the biggest concern for most sellers. Many times, sellers need to get a certain price so that they can afford the home they want to buy. That's completely understandable."

"Let's assume that the market is strong, and you list your house with me. Although I'll give you some guidance, the price we list at is really your decision."

"Now, if your home doesn't get great offers within a couple of weeks in a strong seller's market, we have to ask ourselves what is wrong."

Joe and Maria look at each other with a, "Does that make sense" look and when they are satisfied, turn back to David and nod in agreement.

David continues, "Ok, so in my experience, there are four major reasons a home doesn't sell: a lousy agent, lousy marketing, lousy photos, or a lousy price."

"If I may humbly say so, you can eliminate the first three just by hiring me because I only do first class. You'll get top-shelf, professional service, marketing, and photos with me every time."

"So, what does that leave? Yes, it's rhetorical, but the point is that if we do everything right and your home isn't selling, it's because the price is too high."

Joe cuts in. "David, I appreciate your thoughts, but it sounds like you're already trying to get us to start low on our price to make it easier to sell."

Joe continues. "I've put a lot of work into this place over the years and I want something out of it for my efforts."

"I've installed new kitchen cabinets and granite countertops. We have new appliances as well. Plus, I've remodeled two of the bathrooms."

"Oh, and the basement. I mean, sheesh, I slaved on that thing nights and weekends for a year. What a pain that was!"

David nods in agreement but then says, "Of course, you've put a lot of money and your own labor into this house to make it a home for your family."

"*But this is the tough love part, Joe*. The things you've done to your home are not as important to your buyer as they are to you. I know you don't want to hear that but I not going to patronize you. The price we decide on cannot take into consideration the amount of blood, sweat, and tears you've invested."

David sees the sour look on Joe's and Maria's faces. He pauses and then looks them in the eyes and says,

"We'll get the highest price possible and in the current seller's market, we probably won't have an issue at all. But, my strong advice is to look at your home through the buyer's eyes and not your own."

Secret #5: The improvements you've made to your home are not as important to your buyer as they are to you. It's not fun to hear, but the sooner you accept it, the sooner we get to the true market price. When pricing your home, look at it from the buyer's point of view and not your own.

Joe and Maria look at each other. They know he's right, but it doesn't make it easier to swallow. They feel like they've just taken the red pill in the Matrix movie. They are giving up the fantasy world and have accepted reality as it truly is.

Joe says, "Ya know, if you weren't right, I'd probably ask you to leave."

David winces and responds, "I get that a lot."

Maria offers David more coffee and, now that the uncomfortable topic of price is out of the way, David says, "Ok, now let's look at how we DO come up with the correct market price."

Joe and Maria half-heartedly smile and invite David to continue. But, they are starting to feel like this is the guy.

David begins.

"Ok, so most agents will offer you a CMA, or Comparative Market Analysis free of charge. But just how do they do one?"

"It's actually quite simple when you've done enough of them. It usually starts with the agent's MLS, which stands for Multiple Listing Service if you didn't know."

"He pulls up a search criteria page. Then, he chooses ranges of information around the statistics of your home. For example, if your home was built in 1975, the agent might choose a range of homes built between 1965 and 1985."

"This 20-year window narrows the search to similarly aged homes. It could be tighter or looser depending on the specific situation. As an example, if your home was only a year old, he might not have other newer homes to compare to."

"The agent does this with several items like square footage, number of beds and baths, and the type of home such as single family, condo, or modular."

"Then they use a mapping tool in the MLS to select an area around your home, usually about a half-mile radius, selects "sold" and "for sale" properties, and hits the search button. The results will include on-the-market and sold homes similar to yours but there's still more work to do."

"They look at each result and studies the photos to get an idea of how it compares on things like upgrades. If your home has new granite countertops and a beautiful, remodeled kitchen and the comparable is 90's laminate countertops and light-oak cabinets, they are going to adjust the comparable property down in value."

"They will do this for many things until they feel that there is five or six good, adjusted comparables. This becomes the basis for pricing your home."

"Now, there are other variables, so I don't want to make it sound too simple. A good agent looks at less obvious factors as well. For example, if the agent knows that a new shopping mall, hotel, or hospital will be built nearby in the next year, that would affect value one way or another. He's going to take that into consideration."

Joe's phone rings. He looks at it and says to Maria, "It's Randal."

Maria says, "I don't think we're going to need Randal's services."

Joe nods in agreement and sends a polite text thanking Randal for his time but letting him know they won't be using his services. Joe apologizes for the interruption and asks David to continue.

David ends with, "Well, that's all I wanted to say about that. The point is that the CMA process is good when an agent knows what he's doing, but in the wrong hands, it can be next to useless."

Joe butts in. "What about the instant home valuations you can get on Zillow, Homes.com, or some brokerage website?"

"Ah yes, well, those are known as 'AVM's, or Automated Valuation Models. There are a lot of them but they all suffer from the fact that the computer can't know the local market like an agent who has worked there for years."

"Take the example of the shopping mall being built nearby. That project could affect nearby home values quite a bit, but the computer probably doesn't know about those plans."

"I think the AVMs are an okay place to start for very basic value information, but I'd stick to an experienced agent for the true market value. Also, when an appraiser finally does his job for the eventual buyer, he will have the biggest impact on the sales price of your home. Appraisers do a lot more homework than your agent does to arrive at the best value."

"And, if the price you want is more than the appraisal, the buyer would need to bring the difference to closing. Many buyers aren't prepared to do that. So, in the end, when I do a CMA, I'm trying to figure out what the appraiser will come up with anyway."

Joe and Maria nod as they begin to see the point. Joe squeezes Maria's hand, smiles, and then says, "That is so helpful, thank you."

"You're welcome. My goal is to bring you as much value as possible, not quit until we reach the end zone, and complete my mission."

"I will say this: whatever price we arrive at, it should be in $10,000 increments like $310,000. We're not doing that $309,370 stuff. We're not selling cars here."

"MLS systems aren't set up to search for weird numbers. Nobody searches for homes priced at $309,370 or less. They type in $310,000 or less."

"If you're priced at $299,900 and I search for $300,000 and up, I'll never see your listing. Buyers who initially look at homes priced at $280,000 might stretch to $300,000 and we want them to find your home."

"Yes, sites like Zillow will give you a funky price like $310,594 but it's not the number to use when you actually put the sign in the yard."

"So, that's just one example of the tweaking to maximize the number of people who find your listing."

Joe says, "David, you're making my head spin." Maria chimes in, "Yeah, is there a test at the end?"

David laughs, "No, no test. I just want you to be educated."

"And speaking of educated, let's discuss the agent/client relationship in Colorado.

"It's different in each state but in Colorado I can have one of three relationships with you."

"First is the Agency Relationship, the highest level of responsibility. As an Agent, I advise and advocate for you. That means giving my opinion, negotiating, and informing you. This applies to the buy or sell side."

"As an Agent, my job and my duty are to help you win and win big, in the transaction. As an Agent, I have loyalty only to you. As an Agent, the buyer is merely a customer to me."

"Second is Transaction Broker. As a TB, I don't give you advice or negotiate for you, I'm a paper pusher. I only assist you. No advice on decisions. In fact, the real estate commission won't allow me to do anything else."
"And if I'm representing the buyer AND the seller of the same property at the same time, then I MUST be a TB for both according to real estate commission rules."

"Finally, you could be a Customer. In that situation, I owe you nothing but honesty and in fact, I'm working for the other side. It's the opposite of the agency."

"I must tell you that my policy is to only work as an Agent. If I can't be 100% loyal to you in the transaction, then I'm not interested. The Marine Corps taught me loyalty."

Joe and Maria ask David to go over that again since it's a bit confusing. He does, and they slowly realize the importance of the Agency Relationship.

"So, David, what's the deal with realtors? Is there a difference between an agent and a 'realator'?", Maria asks.

"Well, in the words or Ricky Ricardo from the I Love Lucy show, "I got some 'splainin' to do."

"Here's how it works: a person licensed with the Colorado Real Estate Commission, or CREC, is a 'real estate agent', actually, they're a broker because Colorado wants all agents to have the same level of education and accountability.

Most real estate agents join the National Association of Realtors, or NAR. When they do, they are allowed to use the "designation" of 'Realtor®'".

"The word is 'Real-TOR', though it is commonly said as, 'Real-a-tor', which is incorrect. To be honest, it annoys me but not so much that I'll correct people for it."

"What's the difference?", Joe asks.

"Well, Realtors® are expected to operate at a higher level of ethics because NAR has their own rules that go beyond the CREC rules."

"Also, NAR lobbies Congress for legislation that benefits agents, homeowners, buyers, and sellers."

"And are you a Real-TOR, David?"

"Yes, I am."

Maria says, "Well, thanks for clearing that up and making us look dumb." Then she smiles as if to say, "I'm still going to say 'realator'.

Noted.

Then Joe jumps in and asks, "Ok, David, you've pretty much sold us on you and we know what the average agent does. So, what will you do that's so much better?

The Superhero Agent. Da-Da-Da-Da!

"Ok, now I'll launch into my infomercial. Forgive the marketing rhetoric."

"In addition to all the 'standard' services you're familiar with, I have developed what I call my:"

HPHLS or High Premium Home Listing Service

"I've searched high and low for the top-drawer vendors I need to offer this amazing service and I only work with the best."

David hands Joe and Maria a flier. They look at it dumbfounded, and David begins to read it."

"Every listing gets my unique 24+ point service:"

- Exquisite Listing Photo & Video package provided by one of my amazing professional real estate photographers.

- Stellar Staging Service to help bring out the uniqness of your home to potential buys specifically handpicked by me.

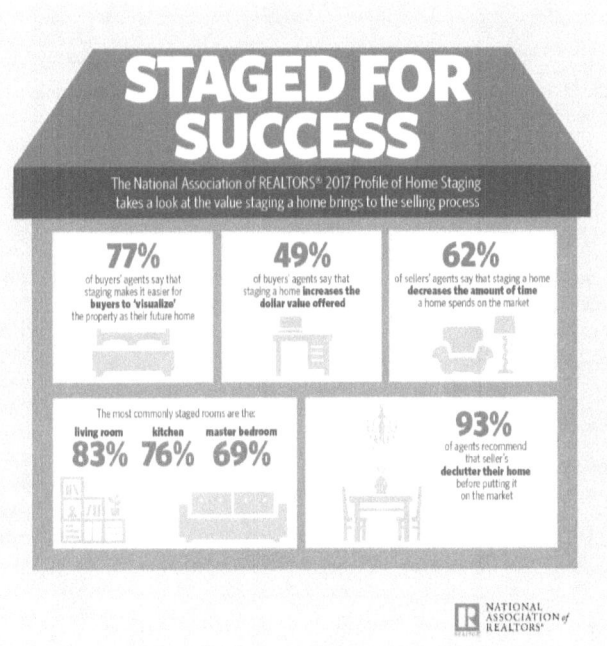

- Window Cleaning. Windows so clean, you have to squint to see the glass.

- Professional showings by Showings.com who will coordinate showings with the buyer agents.

- Buyer agents don't have to reach me, they can set a showing anytime through the Showings.com web site and the instructions you provide.

- Premium Electronic Lockbox by SentriLock that 'knows' every time someone is in the home. It controls the keys to the home and maintains a history. In the information security business, we call it forensics.

- Premium five-foot listing sign on a post that not only has my name and a phone number but also:

  - My photo

  - A toll-free hotline for buyers to call for listing information. This replaces the info sheet and includes a ton more info. Buyers can read it right on their device or print a PDF.

  - A featured ad rider for an incredible lease-with-option-to-purchase program called Home Partners of America.

  - If the buyer qualifies, Home Partners will buy your home for cash and lease it to the buyer. This provides completely different market for folks who want to live in a home but aren't quite ready for a purchase. The cash sale is the best part for you!

- Buyer Loan Spectrum Analysis by one of my preferred lender partners.
  - One of my premium lenders will offer to analyze the types of loans that buyers could use in purchasing your home.
  - Many buyers will already have a pre-approval but for those who don't, we'll offer this service right away.

- Lustrous Lawn Care and Snow Removal. Your yard will be showing-ready at all times!

- Premium Plants and Flowers to make your curb appeal pop.

- HVAC and Water Heater Inspection & Tune Up by a local pro HVAC company

- Roof-Check. Sometimes, we can get you a brand-new roof!

- Grand Garage Door and Opener Service by my list of top-notch door service companies.

- One-Year Home Warranty by First American Home Buyers Protection Corporation. We'll use this as a buyer incentive.

- Savory Scented Candles by Yankee Candles and/or WoodWick Candles to make your home smell delicious! A must for showing time.

"Those are just the things I'm going to do to make your home shine. But wait, there's more! You'll also get:"

- Mega Social Media Blitz to Facebook, Twitter, Instagram, LinkedIn, and MORE.

- Agent to Agent email and Direct Marketing Campaign designed to mobilize the entire real estate community to get them to show and sell your home."

- "A website dedicated only to your home. We use dozens of high-definition and high-impact photos, a virtual tour, proven sales copy language. We also provide links to hundreds of the most visited home buyer websites and social media locations nationally."

- Always Accurate Syndication to Zillow, Trulia, Homes.com, Realtor.com, and MANY others.

- Dedicated Transaction Coordinator who will efficiently manage the entire process beginning to end and provide a single point of contact for your questions or when you need to reach me."

- Flash Status Updates: These are Monday and Thursday updates from my transaction coordinator so that you always know what's going on with your home sale.

"But I'm not done! If you act now, you'll also receive…"

- Encryption and Secure Email Technology protects your sensitive information. I keep your files safe.

- My Super-Secret Laser-Focused Buyer Acquisition System. I have access to tools that allow me to zero in on the buyers we want.

  - For example, I can identify people in the Loveland area between the ages of 60 and 80 with an annual income of $80,000+, who have lived in their current home for 6+ years and are likely to downsize."

"Does that sound like a possible buyer to you, Maria?"

"You can do that?", Maria poses.

"Yep, we'll go after the exact potential buyer market we're interested in. But, I want your sale to be fun too. While I'm working to sell it for you, you'll be living it up."

- <u>FREE mystery deliveries direct to your door each Thursday afternoon. What will show up next!?</u>
  - Movie tickets?
  - Gift cards for restaurants/coffee shops?
  - Wine?
  - Car wash?
  - Tickets to the local music scene?
  - Redbox codes?
  - Free ice cream vouchers?

<u>But I'll warn you, the anticipation might be too much!</u>

"I do reserve the right to substitute service providers when necessary, but they are always top-notch pros."

When David is done listing the services, he takes a deep breath and looks at Joe and Maria. They're stunned. They're just staring at him. Then Maria gets a skeptical look on her face and says,

"Wait a minute, David. That's a heck of list but who's going to pay for all that?"

"I am."

"I pay for it all up front out of my pocket when you list with me. That's how serious I am about your home sale."

Joe jumps in, "Yeah, but what about big repairs that might show up in the inspection? Are you paying for those too?"

"Well, no, but if you <u>do</u> have any 'big' repairs, I'll help you with my awesome contractor referrals to keep costs down. But let's cross that bridge when we come to it."

Maria asks, "Well, how can you do that when you just explained that listing agents don't keep as much of the commission as people think they do?"

"That's why I love **Sellstate**. I keep MUCH more of the commission and it's much, much less expensive to work there than other brokerages."

"That gives me the advantage of treating you guys like royalty. And I wouldn't have it any other way. I'll invest in getting your home showroom ready and you'll get the maximum price for it. Win. Win."

Joe and Maria look at each other knowingly and as if rehearsed, both say at the same time, "You're our guy."

David says, "Well, thank you. Any other questions or concerns? I can give you more time to think about it or we can go over the listing agreement now and start to rock and roll."

"Well, I do have one," says Joe. "How long is the listing agreement for?"

"If I can't sell your home in 90 days in this market, I need to quit real estate. Besides, in the fine print you'll find a FREE 'get out of jail' clause that says you can fire me in 30 days if you're not happy."

"All expenses to that point are mine!"

Maria replies, "I guess we would expect that after all the amazing things you just went over. What an incredible value you offer, David."

"Thanks. I believe you'll be very happy with the results."

Joe and Maria decide to just sign the listing while David is there and when they're satisfied, they walk David to his car. They wave as he drives off.

"Now that's what I'm talking about!" Joe says to Maria.

"Yeah, what a class act," she replies.

They slept well that night knowing they'd hired the right agent and were thrilled to get started!

Conclusion

So, there you have it. The story of one family who started off confused and even cringing a bit but, in the end, found that there really is incredible service in the real estate industry.

They learned a ton about agents, contracts, selling their home themselves, and so much more. They assumed that all agents were alike and that selling a home through one was just too darn expensive.

They discovered that a few, select agents, are on a mission. A mission to be of the highest possible value to you. A mission to be faithful to you and your "why".

I'm one of those agents. And, when selling your home, I WILL complete my mission.

I wish you success in your home-selling pursuit and life,

David McCullough

High Premium Home Listing Service

David McCullough
Sellstate Crossroads Realty
4045 St. Cloud Dr. Suite 100
Loveland, CO 80538

(970) 703-4040
david@davidsellsnoco.com
DavidSellsNOCO.com

WHEN YOU LIST A PROPERTY FOR SALE WITH A REAL ESTATE AGENT, WHAT GOES ON BEHIND THE SCENES?

• "What happens after I sign the contract?"

• "Where does my money go?"

• "Why is it so expensive to sell my home?"

• "What, specifically, is my agent doing to market my home?"

• "Is there a "standard" commission?"

• "Should I use a discount brokerage?"

• "Can't I just sell it myself?"

• "Why is an agent even necessary? What do agents really do, anyway?"

I'll walk you through the process with a fictional family that needs to find a bigger home. When you finish the book, you'll be ready to list your home and know how to do it right!

THE SECRETS TO
SELLING
YOUR HOME

SELLSTATE
CROSSROADS REALTY

THE SECRETS TO
SELLING
YOUR HOME

A REAL ESTATE AGENT REVEALS THE TRUTH

FOR SALE

DAVID MCCULLOUGH